MARK JONES

31 Days to Finding Your Kids' Ministry Mojo

31 Days to Finding Your Kids' Ministry Mojo
By Mark Jones

For book orders/information: www.MrMarksClassroom.com

Volume 1
ISBN 978-0-9899416-4-8
©2017 Mark Jones

Printed in the U.S.A.

Mr. Mark's Classroom
13919 B North May Avenue #139
Oklahoma, City, OK 73134

Endorsements

31 Days to Finding Your Kids' Ministry Mojo translates into 31 solid ideas, suggestions, and wise words from an experienced fellow minister who loves the Lord, children, and families! This is a must read for new ministers and seasoned ministers. Thanks, Mark, for this contribution to our field of ministry to children and families!

Karen Kennemur, PhD
Associate Professor of Childhood Education
Southwestern Baptist Theological Seminary
Fort Worth, Texas

31 Days to Finding Your Kids' Ministry Mojo is a power-packed must-read/must-have children's ministry resource for rookie and seasoned children's ministers alike. Veteran children's minister Mark Jones has provided children's ministry leaders with a practical tool that can be used as a filter to evaluate and ponder the priority given to ministry practices. Whether you are weary and discouraged or are alive and thriving in your children's ministry, after reading this book you are sure to be refueled and refocused to rely on God to help you steer the children's ministry at your church in a direction that is positioned for kingdom growth, connected to families, engaged in encouraging volunteers, and focused on building spiritual foundations in the lives of children.

Dr. Amanda Burkhart
Children's Director
Pleasant Ridge Baptist Church
Morganton, North Carolina

This book is a wealth of information. I am thrilled that Mark has written this to empower leaders. It is relevant for children's leaders in churches of all sizes. I would have benefited from having this resource when I first started in ministry 30 years ago, and I will definitely benefit now. This is years of gathered information and knowledge that only comes from experience.

Thank you, Mark, for your passion to equip leaders to be their best in His service for the Kingdom. I love this book!

Melinda Scurlock
Director of Preschool and Kindergarten Ministry
Houston's First Baptist Church
Houston, Texas

I love Mark Jones' practical approach to kids' ministry and how he shares his knowledge and experiences through the book, *31 Days to Finding Your Kids' Ministry Mojo.*

Mark gives sound and seasoned advice on some of the most important topics facing KidMin leaders today. He encourages us to not only learn but to act. The questions at the end of each day's reading cause us to reflect on the information shared and then to develop action steps that will lead us to specific changes and enhancements that will help us grow our ministries to kids and their families.

Thank you, Mark, for investing in those of us who invest in kids!

Bill Emeott
Childhood Ministry Specialist
LifeWay Christian Resources
Nashville, Tennessee

Table of Contents

Preface IV
Day 1: Shopping for a New Church? 1
Day 2: Three Pillars of Children's Ministry. 5
Day 3: You Teach When You Aren't. 9
Day 4: Ten Lessons in Leadership. 13
Day 5: Doing Ministry Alone 17
Day 6: Simple Steps to Enlisting Leaders 21
Day 7: You Talk Too Much...Seriously 25
Day 8: Guiding Behavior. 29
Day 9: Developing Potential Leaders Starts with You 33
Day 10: Positive Publicity Idea Bank 39
Day 11: Partnering with Your Pastor 43
Day 12: Enlisting Workers Is Driving Me Crazy 47
Day 13: Spectacular Group Outings 51
Day 14: Explaining Salvation to Children 55
Day 15: Is Rotation Sunday School Okay?. 61
Day 16: The Extended Teaching Time Saga Continues. 65
Day 17: Teaching Children? Remember This!. 71
Day 18: Bible Teaching Checklist. 75
Day 19: Should Sixth Grade Be in Youth Ministry?. 79
Day 20: Enlisting Men to Teach Kids. 83
Day 21: How Welcoming Is Your Children's Ministry? 87
Day 22: When a Child Dies 91
Day 23: We Need Help with Enlistment 97
Day 24: Kindergarten vs. First Grade. 101
Day 25: Five Simple Steps to Sharing a Classroom 105
Day 26: Storytelling 109
Day 27: When Kids Become Wild Monkeys. 113
Day 28: Partnering with Parents 117
Day 29: When Teachers Don't Attend Worship 121
Day 30: You are Making a Difference 125
Day 31: The Hidden Blessings of Plan B 129

Preface

Need a Little Mojo in Your Ministry?

Finding your kids' ministry mojo? What is a mojo? It's power that may seem magical and that allows someone to be effective and successful. The empowering that seems magical is really prepared leadership that allows the Holy Spirit to counsel and guide you as you seek to lead kids to Christ. We love kids, but kids' ministry needs a leader who is not scared to deal with adults. God has called me to champion children's ministry just as He has called you. My desire is to help you, or empower you, to be the best leader you can be in kids' ministry.

I want to walk through a daily journaling process to consider areas of leadership needs. I fear I am often too transparent, but those moments seem to bring the most growth in my life. I hope you will be honest and transparent when responding to the different topics I discuss. Carve out time each day to read the brief content and thoughtfully answer the questions. Write other questions and record ideas for your ministry in the space provided. When I read books, I write in the margins and all over the pages. Free yourself to make notes and ask questions as you consider the ideas.

Our ministry focuses on these three groups of people:

- **Children** are so impressionable and want to please adults. We never have to be pushy with the gospel, but we must pray for our kids and faithfully tell them about Jesus.

- **Parents** are not impressed with the crafts their kids make in class. They are impressed when they hear a teacher ask about the child's salvation experience, read how the teacher is praying for their child, and see the teacher building a relationship of love with their child.

- **Teachers** must take advantage of sharing the plan of salvation each month during class. This will help focus children to know the gift of salvation that God is offering them. Share Christ!

As children's ministers, we must be intentional about our efforts to reach families and teach children. How are you structuring your ministry to kids? Are you just playing it by ear? Are you just leading it the way it has always been done? I want you to know some real steps in effective ministry and develop the "why" in your efforts, as well as developing new leadership skills. Your church and families will respond with greater appreciation and focus. This must become the standard by which all programming and activities are filtered.

We are going to consider which are the most important activities. Are you giving prime time to these activities or just some type of filler? I want you to feel like you are actually steering this ministry and it's not steering you. When young parents see the clear plans you have for their kids, they will feel comfortable with the church and making the choice to be involved. Become prepared to reach young adults and guide their children on their spiritual journey.

Mark Jones
Children's Pastor
Quail Springs Baptist Church, Oklahoma City, OK

Website: www.mrmarksclassroom.com
Subscribe for free ideas and activities that teach.

DAY 1
Shopping for a New Church?

A popular trend among parents is to find the "best of" for their kids so that they can feel like good parents. They find the best soccer coach, martial arts instructor, and piano teacher, or simply request the best teacher at their school. Many will pay whatever price to make this happen. Instead of kicking the soccer ball or coaching the team, they will pay someone else to do it. The church will receive the same consideration as young parents look for the best facilities and the best programs such as summer camp, VBS, and Sunday school. We have discovered that 70% of our young adults left church after high school, and now 35% are giving consideration to returning, largely due to having children. They sense the responsibility for providing for the child's spiritual development. Our churches have a small window of opportunity for reaching these young families.

Young adults are not denominationally tied, and they will look around for the church that is doing the best job with kids. They will ask other parents and listen for cues from successful parents they admire. Pastors and children's ministers must take a serious look at

1

what they offer these families. In highly effective churches, you find intentionality and focus. There is no room for half-hearted effort.

Here are a few areas the church must deal with if parents are going to take your church seriously:

- **First Impressions:** Parents will not take your church seriously if their first impression stinks. They are looking for several critical markers. If these items are not in place, you might not get a second chance: the teaching areas and toys must be clean, clutter free, and safe. Be sure the room smells good, and child safety is provided for doors and outlets.

- **Security Systems:** They do not have to be complex, but they must be intentional and supported by workers to make them effective. Simple ideas like signing in kids with parental contact information (such as cell phone numbers) will give assurance to parents. Having windows in the doors so that parents can see in the classroom will help to satisfy anxious parents. Create policies that provide an application with background checks for workers. This will help protect the children and the church. These and other safety ideas can be discussed and implemented through a children's ministry committee.

- **Welcome Children:** Young parents are looking for a church whose teachers respond warmly and responsively to their children. The warm responses from teachers will help to provide the sense of community that young adults are longing to have. By giving individual attention and unconditional love, the teacher will maximize the opportunities to build on spiritual foundations in the life of every child in his or her class. First impressions are vital, but you must clearly communicate the lasting reasons for staying at the church and keeping their children involved. Young adults are seeking a cause to follow and a plan that makes a difference. Clearly communicate your plan for the child's spiritual development.

- **Ministry Objectives:** Provide a clear commitment of spiritual development for kids. Objectives like salvation, Bible skills and serving, just to name a few. To accomplish this plan, children's leaders and teachers need a commitment to the goals and objectives to see themselves as a part of a team that is impacting the lives of children. Then celebrate together as you meet those objectives throughout the year.

Day 1: Questions

1) Is your church a safe place where kids are loved? What needs to be changed?

2) Have you provided objectives and goals to focus on this year and in the years to come?

3) Is your church committed to the spiritual development of children?

DAY 2

Three Pillars of Children's Ministry

Is your church committed to the spiritual development of children? What do you want kids to know and do by the time they move into the youth ministry? Do you want them to be able to quote the lines from "Dave and the Giant Pickle" Christian movie or sing the kids' song "I Want A Hippopotamus for Christmas" in its entirety? I hope not.

Part of your job as a children's ministry leader is to provide a clear vision for the spiritual development of kids in your ministry. Creating a framework that encompasses the following three objectives will go a long way to ensuring that the children graduating out of your ministry have a firm foundation. Additionally, your children's leaders and teachers need a commitment to these three objectives and to see themselves as a part of a team that is impacting the lives of children.

Know Jesus

Children are so impressionable and want to please adults. We never have to be pushy with the gospel, but we must pray for our kids and faithfully tell them about Jesus. Parents are not impressed with the crafts their kids make in class. They are impressed when they hear a teacher ask about the child's salvation experience, read how the teacher is praying for their child, and see the teacher building a relationship of love with their child. Teachers must take advantage of sharing the plan of salvation each month during class. This will help focus children to know the gift of salvation that God is offering them. Share Christ!

Learn Bible Skills

Children must obtain their Bible skills. Parents do not have this on their radar. Whenever I insist that children's workers and parents must help kids obtain their Bible skills, no one pushes back. If kids do not know how to use their Bibles, they will become handicapped Christians who are unable to feed themselves spiritually. Bible skills are not taught in the youth or adult departments; therefore, the responsibility lies squarely on our shoulders. Teachers and parents can easily teach and reinforce learning the books of the Bible, how to use the Bible, and how to memorize verses. These are lifelong skills that will make a huge difference for loving the Word of God and hiding it in their heart. Parents who hear their child reciting verses or finding verses in their Bible are amazed and grateful for the investment the church is making in their child. Teach Bible skills!

Show Children How to Serve

Children are some of the most self-absorbed people. Don't get me wrong; many adults are selfish too. Giving and serving are not inherent traits for children or adults. Children must be shown how to give and serve in a Christ-like manner. It is important to hear about missions, but doing the work of serving others is of much greater value. Kids enjoy opportunities to do for others, and they are hands-on learners. When a child is serving, the focus is on the one being served. The beauty of serving others is not what the child can receive; it is the joy he or she experiences while following in Christ's footsteps. Parents take notice when their children are led to give of themselves and serve others. They appreciate the investment of expanding the child's world from a "me" focus, and they rejoice as they see the child's attitude toward service change.

These characteristics of a preschool and children's ministry must be intentionally put in place. Parents and children alike need to see that these cornerstones of children's ministry are incorporated throughout all of the areas of your ministry. When young parents see the clear plans you have for kids, they will feel comfortable with church and making the choice to be involved.

Day 2: Questions

1) Which one of these three objectives is the hardest one for you to see within your ministry? What can you do to change this?

2) What are you already doing that supports these three objectives?

3) Would a young family coming in the door this Sunday feel comfortable with your church? Would they readily see the importance of these objectives in your ministry?

DAY 3

You Teach When You Aren't

Are you and your teachers practicing intentional leadership? We all want to have an effective ministry. We take the time to look at curriculum, enlist teachers, pray for those in our ministry, and prepare for the lesson that we are about to present – all of which are so very important. But do you know you can be sending messages without saying a word? Do realize you can affect the relationships you have with children without even saying a word? God works through relationships, so you need to be building relationships, not creating distance between you and the children.

Here are five points that will help you teach to your full potential and keep you truly invested in your ministry:

You Teach Through the Environment

Many teachers forget that cluttered rooms, tattered curtains, and messy walls send a message that teaching kids is not important. Is your ministry space inviting to children? Does your classroom's neat appearance ad clean environment show that you care about the children? Take an honest look at your classroom to determine if the setup is conducive to your teaching, age appropriate, and inviting to those who enter. If you share the space with others throughout the week, call a "roommates" meeting. Work together to make your room speak to children of your love for them. Clean up clutter. Replace tattered bulletin boards and place toys in bins. Store extra materials and curriculum inside the cabinets, not strewn about on the counter. Take pride in your room. Cleanliness will speak volumes to the children who enter your door.

We Teach Through Our Facial Expressions

Your eyes are called the windows of the soul for a reason. Do your eyes speak love or do they speak distance and disapproval? Use your eyes to communicate to the children that you care, you are invested in the conversation with them, and you simply enjoy spending time with them. Wink across the table to reassure a child who is uncertain about their presence in your room. Smile and say, "I love you" and let those words shine through your eyes. Your eyes are a great tool of affirmation – use them.

We Teach Through Our Body Language

What kind of vibe do kids get from you? Are you walking calmly around the room, taking the time to greet the children at eye level? Or are you towering around the room with your hands on your hips? Your body language can communicate positive or negative feelings to those around you. If you stand with your arms crossed the entire time, what is the message you are sending to children? If you sit slumped over in your chair while the other teacher is telling the Bible story, do children understand that the Bible is the living, breathing Word of God? Use your body language to communicate to the children in the room how excited you are to spend time with them, and how important it is to learn from the Bible.

We Teach Through Our Voice Inflections and Volume

Your voice can be used to draw children into a story or be that warm, welcoming presence at the door. Remember, while some children may be accustomed to a higher noise volume, a child not used to loud noises can be frightened by a big, booming voice or overwhelming classroom noise. When trying to get the children's attention in a classroom, don't try to talk above the crowd. Instead, try to whisper to get their attention and see what happens. Another great tool is asking the children to clap if they can hear your voice. Continue asking the question until all of the children are clapping. It's a great way to get the volume in your classroom back to a manageable level and help the children to regain their focus. When teaching, speak clearly and distinctively. No one can understand when someone is mumbling or trying to win an award for being the fastest voice in the West. When you are giving instructions, it can be beneficial to only give one step at a time. Kids are the priority in your classroom, so don't spend your time conversing with the other adults in the room. There is plenty of time to catch up with your friends once the teaching session is over. Instead, use the time to show the children in the room that they are the priority; engage in conversation with them. God will use your efforts to provide teachable moments. Use your voice as a tool in your classroom; it's a great one.

We Teach Through Our Dress

Do you wear colorful clothes or are you straight out of the Adam's Family, always in black? Remember that your appearance reflects your priorities. Be well groomed, not disheveled. Teaching kids requires that your clothes be comfortable. This is not the time to wear that super cute, so-in-style new pencil skirt or that tight across the shoulders jacket. Your clothes need to be flexible so that you are able to get down on the children's level and interact with them.

Day 3: Questions

1) In which area do you need to improve?

2) Which area do your teachers struggle with the most?

3) From a child's perspective, how are your teachers currently presenting themselves?

DAY 4

Ten Lessons in Leadership

Being on church staff for 20 years has rewarded me with beautiful friendships and divine moments of personal and spiritual growth. I have worked with children, teachers, and pastors who have taught me valuable lessons. Each lesson has become a story that has shaped my view of leadership today. Here are ten principles I have learned:

Recognize that inflexible leadership fails when it is time to make needed changes.

1. If you are still doing the same things you did when you started in kids' ministry, you are stunting your growth. You need people to take your place in ministry tasks. "I" am a limited resource. Multiply yourself in others.

2. Move up to a new level of leadership. Seek to go ahead of your followers and begin building a road your ministry will go down. Road construction can take a long time.

3. Identify the men and women under you, and the strengths

they possess. Begin delegating roles of service, and build an army of capable and reliable workers.

4. Don't criticize people or ministries who follow a different course. God may be using them in unique ways to reach and minister to others.

5. Be honest and recognize what you don't know. Identify resources and people to help you learn.

6. Allow yourself room to be wrong and to grow from your mistakes. See your mistakes as opportunities to grow and become a better leader.

7. Anticipate problems and help create solutions.

8. Don't let murmurings control your leadership. Don't listen to picking and critical unconstructive comments. You cannot make everyone happy.

9. Be a risk taker. Try new things. They won't all work, but some of them will. You will discover what is usable and effective in working with your people.

Begin praying for a vision for what God wants to do in and through you. Gather people together and allow them to dream with you. Show them your heart and passion for the work. Prioritize and organize yourself to move forward and make a big impact on those you lead and teach. Soon, your followers will have a passion for the work, too.

Day 4: Questions

1) Which one of these is the hardest for you to put into action? Why is this area so difficult for you? Take a few moments and ask God to help you grow in this area.

2) Identify someone who can serve as a mentor for you. They should be someone who can objectively help you evaluate your areas of ministry and keep you accountable, not just someone who will be a great cheerleader. Make sure it isn't someone in your church or in your family.

3) Write the names of four people in your ministry, their areas of strength, and how they their strengths can build up the ministry.

DAY 5

Doing Ministry Alone

It can be easy to fall into the mode of being a control freak. You want your ministry to be the very best ministry that you can make it. You have a specific way that you want something done, but when others help, it is just not quite right. As a children's ministry leader, you will exhaust yourself trying to do it all alone.

I know your pain; it's happened to me. You get an idea and want to run with it. It's too hard to communicate, and you're ready to get started anyway. The problem is, you're the only one doing it. I applaud creativity. I most often cannot sleep all night because I get an idea and have to consider it. Most of the time I get so attached to the idea you would think I fathered it. It's almost like it's my baby and I would be terribly offended if someone called my baby ugly. Well, you know what I mean. Look at Ephesians 4:11-12: *"It was he who gave some to be apostles, some to be prophets, some to be evangelists, and some to be pastors and teachers, to prepare God's people for works of service."* Notice it says nothing about children's ministers, but it does say pastor (shepherd). You are an extension of the pastor, and represent him to the children's ministry. Since God has called you to pastor, or shepherd, these children, you will need an army of volunteers to do it well. You are probably the best children's teacher, and you should be, but your role has changed. You are leading now.

It is your responsibility to your kids, parents, workers, pastor, and above all, God, to understand your role as leader. You will have plenty of times to be the classroom teacher, but now you must become the coach of a winning team. Here are five steps to success:

1) Take a mental inventory of workers' strengths and weaknesses. Pray for wisdom and begin fitting people into the positions that best match their strengths.

2) Chart in a notebook all the positions needed currently, and then write in all the names of volunteers. You might need someone in a place you overlooked, or you are possibly overstaffed in another area. Having this written down will help you from feeling overwhelmed.

3) Ask the hard questions:
   - Do we need this program?
   - Am I trying to do too much, too soon?
   - What are the prime attendance times, and are the goals we have being met during these times?
   - Is there anyone who needs to be trained or moved to another level of leadership (or fired)?

4) Plan a meeting with key leaders to share your ideas and passion for what you want to accomplish. Include a deacon if possible. He'll speak of this among the deacons favorably, and they will naturally be informed. Invite your leaders to push back so your idea can be

stronger. Don't be threatened by criticism or questions. Write them down and begin working on solutions. By conducting regularly scheduled meetings, you will invite people to begin to invest in their own leadership. It will then be a natural progression for them to want to participate in it. This is an integral part of equipping the people.

5) Foster relationships with your people. God doesn't write things in the sky to direct us, He works through relationships: our relationship with Him as we learn, and our relationships with others as we serve. It would make sense that Satan is also working through relationships. Maybe you need to go to lunch with a worker and just talk about your families and the things you have in common. Put friendship first because the person is most important.

If you continue on the path you know is wrong, you will soon quit. Don't let Satan defeat you. Allow people to make mistakes and try things. Coach them, resource their ideas and celebrate by affirming them in spoken or written words.

Day 5: Questions

1) What are two things that you can release and let someone else take over? Remember, the work may not be exactly how you would do it, but God will still use their efforts.

2) Who should you ask to be a part of your leadership team?

3) Who are three people in your ministry that you need to invite to lunch so that you can strengthen your relationship?

DAY 6
Simple Steps to Enlisting Leaders

Here I am in January again and everyone is wishing me a Happy New Year. Yes, I'm all for happiness but I have a problem. Since we promoted kids in August and started a new Sunday school year, I still don't have workers for one of my classrooms. I have called many people, and have heard from one husband, "Don't call my wife again; she's taking a break." I honored his request of course.

Finding subs has been a hassle and I find myself questioning God, "Why can't I find teachers for this class?" So I revisited some steps to enlisting leaders for encouragement.

At some point in your ministry, you will face the same issue. Here is my list of thirteen things to do when you are still looking for volunteers.

1. Pray. Seek God's guidance. Ask Him for the person to fit the needed ministry position. Be still and listen for His response. Pray for the person even before you make the first contact.

2. Make a phone call to set up a time to meet in person. Don't ask in the church hallway unless you want to be avoided like the plague. (That's the truth!)

3. Be prepared to share written information about the class, including written characteristics about the age group they will be teaching. Provide a leader guide and class roll.

4. No bait and switch. Discuss honestly the qualifications and the expectations for the leadership position. The worst thing you can do is try to downplay the commitment involved. It is always best to be forthright about everything the position requires.

5. Explain the process of screening leaders for the protection of the children. Share your testimony and ask them to share their testimony with you. Don't ever assume that you can skip this step just because someone is kind and involved in the church.

6. Keep the meeting brief, but allow time for questions. Answer questions honestly. Again, this isn't the time to sugarcoat or downplay expectations.

7. Invite the leader to assist and observe you during a session before making a decision.

8. Pray together. Ask them for specific prayer requests. Don't just pray about their decision to volunteer.

9. Leave your contact number and information so that you can be contacted easily.

10. Set a date to follow up, or the answer may never come.

11. Send a note, text, or email thanking the potential leader for his or her time and consideration. Assure the individual that you are praying for him or her.

12. Follow up as planned.

13. Accept the answer. If yes, set a start date and provide encouragement, training, and support. If no, accept the answer graciously. You don't want the individual to accept the position and then rarely show up, or quit in a few weeks. If the person says no, it might be the beginning of a process through which God will call that person in time.

Day 6: Questions

1) What other ideas would you add?

2) Which one of these tips is the hardest for you to do? Why?

3) What should you do to keep from feeling frustrated when a volunteer says no?

DAY 7

You Talk Too Much...Seriously

I have witnessed and worked with the most loving teachers who care deeply for the kids and their families, but they have one tragic flaw – they talk nonstop. How do you politely tell Miss Jabber-jaws to close her mouth? This might sound harsh but kids need to have the opportunity to talk. More importantly, kids need to be heard. This requires teachers to take the time to stop talking and listen.

Think back to a time when someone listened to you. Maybe it was your mom or grandmother. You knew they were listening, so you started giving all the good details. This is how the children in your classroom will respond once they know you want to hear what they have to say.

Many people are frustrated because they don't have anyone to listen to them. They may even feel that whatever they have to say is of no value to their spouse or boss. Kids feel the same way. Many kids hear certain phrases far too often. "Not right now." "Can't you see I'm busy?" "Later." "Don't bother me, this is important." Now is the time to start listening to our children. So here is a question for you to consider: do you talk *to* children or do you talk *with* children? Many children have adults who want to give them advice and teach them, while not listening to their opinions and feelings. Our kids might independently discover solutions to many things if they could talk about their issues. Think about it; adults often "think out loud" as a form of problem solving. Children do as well.

Children will also turn to dramatic behavior in order to be heard. Consider your classroom of kids. You may be busy trying to accomplish everything in the curriculum on a limited time schedule. What if you did one thing less and allowed space in your schedule for kids to talk more? Children's behavior would be more respectful and friendly because the teacher is not rushed and genuinely wants to hear what they have to say.

Never underestimate the power of authentic relationships with children. Often we become so focused on making sure we have the coolest illustration, best music video, or most well laid-out classroom. Your work with kids is done through the relationships you build, not through the classrooms you have painted and decorated. You do need places to meet and study the Bible, as well as activities to drive the lesson home, but meeting places and additional activities are not more important than the relationships.

Try these ideas for building relationships through listening:

- Don't interrupt. Take the time to be still and listen to what the children have to say.

- Repeat back phrases. This allows the child to know you were listening, and to add additional information if they would like.

- Maintain eye contact. You would question if someone were truly listening to you if they failed to make eye contact with you. Children are no different.

- Listen for their feelings. When children know that you are invested in the conversation, they will begin to open up and share deeper thoughts.

Don't just consider what happens inside the classroom. Consider ways that you can maintain the relationship and let the child know you remember the conversation and care to continue the dialogue. Some good follow-up ideas might include sending a card in the mail, texting a Bible verse, or speaking encouragement to them outside the classroom. These actions show you were listening.

The bottom line is that children need to know you are as interested in really knowing who they are as you are in teaching them the lesson. Choosing to take the time to listen to a child talk will accurately relay the message that you treasure them as an individual, and are willing to take the time necessary to invest in the relationship.

Day 7: Questions

1) What are some ways you promote conversations with kids?

2) What are some barriers that could prevent you from really listening to kids? What are some ways that you can eliminate or reduce these barriers?

3) What are some additional ways that you can follow up on conversations with kids?

DAY 8

Guiding Behavior

Discipline and behavior are two of the most challenging parts of teacher interactions with students. Effective classroom management is vital to a good learning environment. Let's take a look at why discipline is difficult, what discipline really is, and how we can appropriately guide behavior.

Why Do Teachers Avoid Discipline?
- They don't know what to do.
- They have not prepared adequately for the session.
- They are too busy.
- They want the children to be happy.
- They believe giving in once won't hurt.
- They are just trying to get through the session.
- They lack a personal relationship with the children.

The teacher sets the tone for the classroom. To create an atmosphere of positive discipline, the teacher must be a positive role model and set the example. Children will follow the teacher's lead.

What Is the Goal of Discipline?

The goal of godly discipline is to guide children to make the correct choice. A child who can evaluate the situation and still choose to make the right choice, even when a teacher isn't directly supervising, is a child who is benefiting from godly discipline and growing in his or her spiritual journey. Self-discipline, where the child will learn to create boundaries based on a sense of the impact of good and bad choices, should be the targeted outcome.

What Is the Process of Discipline?

The word *discipline* describes the process of helping a child grow. We are given a biblical example of this in Luke 2:52: *"Jesus grew in wisdom, stature and favor with God and man."* The process of developing a sense of discipline, or self-control, allows children to grow in what and how they think, how they treat their bodies, and how they relate to God and the people around them. Focus on discipline as training. Children should receive one warning, and then the consequence for a bad choice. To help children acquire the skill of self-discipline, talk through decision-making with them. Coach the children as they interact with others. Step back and allow them the opportunity to make the right decision and stand firm with the consequence if they don't.

*Remember to have age-appropriate expectations for the children in your classroom. These children will act like children; don't forget to enjoy them.

What Are the Attitudes of Discipline?

The teacher should view his or her role as that of a trainer, not a punisher. Use language that encourages children. Let them know you believe they can make the right choice. When children are frustrated, offer words or questions to help them describe their feelings. Help kids to not give up. God has given them a free will so that they can make the right choice, even if they have made the wrong choice in the past.

What Is the Environment of Discipline?

A room that is set up for age-appropriate learning and is clear of distractions will go a long way towards encouraging the appropriate classroom environment. Classroom scenarios that provide opportunities for choices will foster self-discipline. A room that is full of affirmation, teacher praise, celebration, cooperation with others, and self-directed learning will round out the equation.

*When guiding children towards appropriate choices, give positive feedback. Don't use phrases such as "You're going to listen, even if it kills you!"

What Part Does Punishment Play in Discipline?

The goal of discipline is not to punish children; the ultimate goal is self-discipline. Utilize facing the consequences of bad choices. Discipline becomes a system of consistent choices, consequences, and boundaries. Avoid negative comments, labeling, and belittling. The question every teacher should ask is not, "How can I punish this child for what he did?" but rather, "What can the child learn from this situation?"

Day 8: Questions

1) What are some ways that you can specifically encourage self-discipline within your classroom?

2) What is the most difficult part of fostering self-discipline in your classroom?

3) How can you encourage your teachers to adopt these principles in their classroom?

DAY 9
Developing Potential Leaders Starts with You

In my mad search for directors and teachers for Sunday school, I found a winner and enlisted her right away. Things didn't quite go as planned though. Here is a play-by-play of the decline in morale of the promising teacher:

Beginning of the year
- Excited and wanting ideas
- Needed more teachers
- Always on time and prepared
- Smiled and radiated joy
- Worked in children's events and on committees
- Gave it her best shot

Middle of the year
- Enthusiasm began waning
- Began to have a look of defeat
- Made less time for meetings
- Started dropping hints of quitting

End of the Year
- Lost her joy in serving
- Resigned when she fulfilled the year commitment

She shared some responsibility, but I have full ownership for the outcome of this particular teacher. We wrestle with keeping volunteers happy and productive as well as motivated and connected. Leadership development is about an outcome. Jesus, through His ministry, showed us an incredible model of investing in and developing leaders. So how can we develop potential leaders? We have to build the foundation, just like Jesus did.

Make It Mean Something
Churches cannot hire everyone, so we are driven to hunt for volunteers. As a volunteer, I asked myself, "Why am I serving?" There are many reasons why people volunteer. "I want to serve Jesus." "I love kids." "I have so much fun." "I want them to accept Christ." Like most people, I spend my week in meetings, pleasing my employer, and helping churches and other employees. I look forward to being in the classroom with the kids - making a difference in their lives. The main reason people say they choose to volunteer is, "It brings meaning to my life." People with this as their motivation are potential leaders who are ready to serve.

Volunteers want to do something that is meaningful. People who are looking for a meaningful experience want you to give a clear and compelling purpose. Happy volunteers are crystal clear on their ministry's purpose. They can tell you not only why their ministry group exists, but also why it is important. For an important cause, leaders will give unselfishly and thank you for it.

Involve Volunteers as Much as Possible
If you miss this, you will drive your volunteers nuts. On one hand, volunteers are busy and juggling multiple priorities. On the other

hand, they desperately want to have input into the direction and development of the ministry. Simply donating funds or following staff-made plans fails to incite long-term motivation. Leadership teams that start with a blank paper, listen to the heart of the minister, and then to each other's hearts will develop a collaborative vision and plan for the future as a team.

Don't Waste Their Time

Our volunteers develop a sensitive nose for the hopelessly under-resourced project. Starving projects need to be pruned from the ministry project list.

We can become leaders who are trying to staff and support too many ministry projects. Some of these lesser important projects simply need to be eliminated. Call it good church hygiene. Regularly take a look at each project and decide if it can be resourced or reshaped or discontinued. When all sub-ministries run dangerously close to the bone, volunteers become less motivated. Maybe you need a "stop doing" list as much as you need a "to do" list.

Celebrate with Meaningful Moments

I have celebrated my volunteers with a meal where I told them how I felt about the ministry and about their sacrifice to make a difference. I have hosted many meetings in my home, never forgetting to appreciate each person and share my heart for the ministry being done. I have recognized people from the pulpit, during deacon's meetings, at finance meetings, and especially during meetings where children were present and I could love on them. It is easy to brag about people to their family and friends. Take the time to do it.

Stop Hogging the Ball

Any ball player knows how much fun it is to play with a "ball hog" (sarcasm implied). That player is silently communicating he doesn't trust you to do something good with the ball. Eventually, you just want to sit down. How often do you really entrust your volunteers with doing the most important part of ministry?

I can remember wanting to take a part of a ministry that I was well equipped to do, and in which I had many years of experience. I volunteered only to hear, "No, I would rather you not be responsible for it, but you can do most of the work. Just clear everything through me before you do anything." I was very disappointed, unmotivated, disliked the project, disliked the leader, felt second rate or not good enough, and desperately wanted to quit. All of these feelings surfaced because the leader chose to be a "ball hog." Are you being a "ball hog" with anything? Try being the coach and a cheerleader.

Using these five methods will empower your volunteers and give them the staying power so that they can have satisfaction in their respective roles. Your satisfaction, your journey, has come from pouring your life into your ministry. Our volunteers can't see that far down the road. We have to support and assist them until they too begin to see the fruition of their efforts.

Day 9: Questions

1) What is your motive when enlisting volunteers? Filling a position or helping someone find their God-given potential?

2) What are some specific ways that you can begin to celebrate meaningful moments with your volunteers?

3) Are you being a "ball hog?" What tasks do you need to entrust to your volunteers now?

DAY 10

Positive Publicity Idea Bank

So often we hear about the day-to-day aspects of childhood ministry. "There were five poopy diapers during ETC today." "Oh, vacation Bible school is almost here. You know they are going to be asking for volunteers." "What time can we drop off our kids again?" If you aren't careful, you can get bogged down with all of the negative communication being thrown at you. Likewise, if all people hear about children's ministry is the negatives or pleas for assistance, they will begin to have a negative perception of your ministry as a whole. Positive publicity is crucial to a healthy, thriving children's ministry.

In the heat of preparations, it can be tough to come up with creative and positive ways to promote your ministry. Here's an idea: have chalkboards hanging on your office wall. Use them as the parking lot (or think tank) for all of your positive publicity ideas. You often think of really terrific ideas to implement in children's ministry, and if you don't write them down, you will forget.

Here are some ideas to get you started:
- Create inexpensive refrigerator magnets.

- Compile a children's ministry photo gallery to post on a bulletin board and your church website.

- Choose a slogan for your event or program – some examples are "Serving Children with Joy" or "Teach a Child, Grow a Life"

- Provide the church secretary with a steady stream of information.

- Put posters around the church. Move them around often.

- Ask your music minister to use a song the children know. Teach it to the congregation.

- Create a prayer team.

- Display children's artwork.

- Place a TV in a high traffic area and play a pre-recorded children's session.

- Interview a children's worker during the worship service.

- Host an open house so that the congregation can see the children's space.

- Create a mission statement for your childhood ministry.

- List your staffing needs monthly in church publications and emails.

Day 10: Questions

1) What are some events that you need to create positive publicity for?

2) What are some misconceptions that people commonly have about those events?

3) Pick one of the events and brainstorm three methods of positive publicity.

DAY 11

Partnering with Your Pastor

Your pastor can be an incredible advocate for childhood ministry. It's so important to view your relationship with your pastor as a partnership. You are working towards the same goal of furthering God's kingdom. Don't let Satan steal the blessing of being able to work alongside your pastor as you minister to those in your church.

Here are ten ways you can build your partnership with your pastor and safeguard against potential discord.

1. Pray for your pastor. Leadership takes a toll on us all; be a prayer warrior in support of your pastor.

2. Always respect and honor your pastor publicly and privately. If you disagree with the pastor, ask to sit down and talk with him about it in private. Pray before you meet with the pastor and go in with an open mind. If, at the end of the meeting, you still disagree, do so with respect and continue to honor him both publicly and privately.

3. Get to know your pastor outside the church environment. Invite his family over for dinner at your house or out to eat after church service. Knowing someone personally helps you to work well with them professionally.

4. Talk to your pastor. Open communication is a key foundation for any relationship. Regularly sit down with your pastor and talk about the church, your ministry, and non-church related things. Avoid exaggerating the facts.

5. Make sure your vision for the childhood ministry matches the pastor's vision for the church. Communicate your vision with your pastor just as you do with your volunteers.

6. Be the children's champion before your pastor, but do not forget to do so respectfully. Remember that your job is to know the development of children and how to minister to them; your pastor's job is to minister to the church as a whole. You will have to remind him what is best for children at times. Choose not to take his decisions as a reflection of his disinterest in children or the value he places on them.

7. Inform your pastor about what is happening in the children's ministry and with the families within your ministry. Allow him to celebrate victories and know disappointments with you. Stay away from dramatic behaviors.

8. Include your pastor whenever possible in children's events, but respect his calendar. Including him in your

events will help him to see what is going on within your ministry and join in your excitement. His presence will also communicate to parents and children how much he values them and the ministry.

9. Be your pastor's champion in front of the children. Children are watching you to see your viewpoint of the pastor. Show them how to treat a pastor.

10. Invite your pastor to leadership events, but accept no as a reasonable answer. Remember that pastors are pulled in many different directions too, so don't allow his negative answer to negatively affect your perception of your pastor.

Day 11: Questions

1) What are three specific ways that you can pray for your pastor?

2) Which one of these is the hardest for you to put into action? What are two specific steps you can take to get started?

3) Write down two specific events (children's events or leadership events) that you can ask your pastor to attend.

DAY 12

Enlisting Workers Is Driving Me Crazy

Enlisting workers is a big task regardless of the size of your church. At my church, we promoted Sunday school three weeks ago, we kicked off Wednesday nights two weeks ago, and I still need workers. I'm about to pull out my last three hairs! You would think in a church that is the size of many Oklahoma towns, I would have plenty of workers. Wrong.

I need to replace at least five workers that have already quit. Seriously? (That's what I wanted to say when they called me.) The week before promotion Sunday, a new worker wanted to drop by and see the classroom where she would be teaching. I agreed and we met. I walked her to the room and introduced her to the workers celebrating their last Sunday. They were so kind to show her around so I left them to chat. I was shocked when I got a call on Monday that the new worker was quitting before she ever started. That was followed by another call, her co-teacher, who also quit before ever starting.

I have no idea what was said when I left the room but my frustration peaked along with my blood pressure. I'm trying to fill the last remaining places, and now I'm starting over with a few new places because someone pulled out yesterday and another one quit today. It makes me start to wonder, have I got cooties or something? Why are these teachers quitting? Why can't people enjoy teaching kids as much as I do? Enlisting workers is driving me crazy!

I desperately want to love my workers, train my workers, appreciate my workers, and brag about my workers, but they need to stay on board first. Although this does remind me, there are a couple hundred workers in place and serving faithfully. So if you're like me, let's stop pouting and whining. Don't you dare whine to the pastor; he doesn't want to hear all that. If he asks, be honest, positive, and confident. No drama. Drama gives us a bad reputation. Now is the time to let our faith show. I truly believe God cares for His church and will fit it together perfectly. So make this promise with me:

I promise to:

- Not complain about the work God has called me to do.

- Pray to the Lord of the harvest for laborers needed.

- Schedule substitute teachers to serve for a week or month, and then leave them alone.

- Encourage and affirm present teachers who are doing a great job.

- Never confront someone about teaching while the person is at church to worship.

- Continue to make calls and send texts and emails to invite workers to join my team.

- Write articles and reports in church publications about my vision and successes.

- Recognize other places to serve in the kid's ministry besides teaching.

- Have realistic expectations, healthy training, and positive feedback for teachers.

- Thank God for every teacher He provides, because they are a gift from Him.

Day 12: Questions

1) Consider Galatians 6:9-10, Matthew 9:37-38, and 1 Corinthians 12:17-19. How do these verses apply to seeking volunteers in your ministry?

2) What area of your ministry seems to be the hardest to fill with volunteers?

3) What are some things you could change about this area that would help it to be more volunteer friendly while still meeting the purpose of the area?

DAY 13

Spectacular Group Outings

Taking a group of kids out on an excursion can be an incredible time of bonding and team building. It can also be a bit of a logistical nightmare if you don't properly plan in advance. A few months ago, my church took a group of second and fourth graders to a fun pizza place with lots of entertainment and games to play. During our terrific time, I took some notes on how to have the best experience when traveling with a group of kids.

Here are several things to consider when you are preparing to take a group of children out for an event:

- Plan ahead by calling, reserving, and preparing everything, including informing parents with a take-home note. You should make a site visit and physically see the room or space you reserve, and think about how the number of kids and adults will fit in the space. If eating, consider how people could orderly and safely be dismissed to get their food and drink with minimum spillage. Remember that one of your biggest concerns will be ensuring

51

that there are adults with the kids all the time while everyone eats. Don't forget to have a plan in place for when children want to go back for seconds. If you are going to a larger location, such as an amusement park, decide well in advance how you will keep track of the children. Will you all travel as one big group or will you break up into smaller groups? Will you assign specific children to specific sponsors? Consider having children wear wristbands with a contact number in case they get separated from the group.

- Sometimes you may not know all of the names of the children in the group. Think about providing nametags for every child. Brightly colored tags with the first name boldly printed would be helpful. The adult sponsors need to wear nametags too. Times outside the classroom and church are important for getting to know each other better. Knowing everyone's name is vital.

- At our event, while the children were in the game area, we had a frantic race against the clock. Everyone had 45 minutes to play all the games they wanted and gather all the tickets they could for those incredible, one-of-a-kind prizes to choose from at the end. Kids were running around like mad men, dropping their coats, game cards, and tickets. It was great to watch, but was a bit disconcerting as well. Consider what portions of your event will be most hectic, and then have a plan in place to make it as stress-free as possible. Have children go to the restroom before entering the game room, splitting up for various activities, and again before they get on the buses.

- When it is time to leave, gather in the meeting room again to count the children. Have more than one person count heads. Call roll to line up and board the bus. Recount everyone on the bus before leaving. If you are taking multiple vehicles, have a list of who is in each vehicle and have the head sponsor of each vehicle take roll once everyone is settled in their seat. Keep a master list with you. The thought of leaving a child behind should scare the bee-gee-bees out of you. I know it does me.

- Have activities for children to do during the ride. Singing on the bus is always a big deal. You don't want to get caught listening to some crazy rap songs. Rack your brain before you leave and have a list of those hilarious songs you always used to sing on the bus. Write them down so that you don't forget during the ride. Whether the drive is short or long, your memory will be shorter.

Traveling with kids can be a bit of a daunting task without a good plan in place. Don't miss out on the opportunity to have an incredible event with the kids in your ministry because you are unprepared. Safety should be foremost in your mind, but remember your primary objective of providing an opportunity for your group to get together and grow closer to each other. You want fun to be had by all.

Day 13: Questions

1) What concerns you most about taking a group on a trip?

2) What additional tips can you think of for your specific group when taking them on an outing?

3) What event can you begin planning, and what are five specific things you need to take into account as you prepare?

DAY 14

Explaining Salvation to Children

Whether you are a parent or a children's minister, explaining salvation to children can be an intimidating task. You want to make sure that the child understands the weight of the decision he or she is committing to when asking Jesus to be Lord and forgive his or her sins. There is also the concern that you don't want to pressure children into a decision they aren't ready to make. Many parents I have talked to have expressed a great deal of anxiety when discussing explaining salvation to their children. Emotions range from excitement and elation to feeling under-prepared, inadequate, and untrained. As a children's minister, you will probably feel a great deal of excitement and joy, but you might also feel a little unsure about how to best present the gospel to a child. "Am I explaining with words the child will understand?" "Are the parents pressuring the child?" "Are they discouraging the child?" "Is the experience intimidating or welcoming?"

Let's talk about some key points for leading a child to Christ. I have the opportunity to lead kids to Christ on a regular basis. I consistently use the same approach and it always allows us to have a conversation.

Some key concepts to utilize as you discuss salvation with a child are:

1. Welcome the child with energy, excitement, and acceptance. If meeting in my office, I show them my collection of antique toys and pictures of my family, which gives them a few minutes to become comfortable.

2. Always invite the parents to join you and be involved. Be cautious, and don't let the parents answer for the child.

3. Begin by praying. Invite the Holy Spirit to bring understanding to all in the meeting. Be sensitive to where the child is in his or her spiritual journey.

4. Use one-verse evangelism or another method that is appropriate for the child's developmental level. I always sit next to the child and write the verse and illustrations on a sheet of paper.

5. Remember to avoid using cursive writing. Many children aren't familiar with cursive handwriting, so eliminate potential blocks and print instead.

6. You can have the child copy the verse you are talking about. Use this as a potential red flag when the child can't copy the verse. There is a good chance that he or she isn't developmentally ready to understand all of the foundational truths of salvation. Begin the conversation with an early end in mind. You can schedule the next meeting to talk again. Give the child some time.

7. Ask questions about the components of salvation to

see if the child comprehends. Remember, don't ask questions that require only yes or no answers. Ask open-ended questions that will help you determine the child's knowledge of these key components:

8. What is sin and how sin affects our relationship with God. Don't dumb down what sin is. The child needs to understand why sin separates us from God.

9. Understanding that the child is a sinner.

10. Why Jesus had to die to save us from our sins and why He was the only one who could.

11. The need for God to be the boss of our lives once we accept salvation.

12. Avoid big words or churchy language. Explain words like "resurrection" when they come up. When talking about lordship, use the concept of Jesus being their boss. Most children understand that a boss has the right to tell you what to do, and the need to follow what a boss says.

13. No need to push a child. If the child isn't clued in or is easily distracted during your discussion time, it might be an indication that he or she isn't ready yet. Plan more appointments to meet and continue the discussion if the child is not ready at this time. Be an advocate for the child if the parent is pushing for a decision and the child isn't ready.

14. If the child is comfortable praying on his or her own, let them so. Remember, the child doesn't have to repeat a prayer; the prayer simply needs to be a heart-felt prayer of repentance and acceptance of God's leadership. After a child prays for salvation, reassure them that God heard their prayer and forgiven their sin.

15. Take a tour of the baptistery and discuss what happens there. Set a date to be baptized.

16. Provide blank invitations to attend the child's baptism. Children want to invite family and friends to come.

17. Provide a new Christians' class; give the child a journal, a Bible reading plan.

18. Follow-up with parents to answer any questions they might have.

Plan some meeting dates to train parents to talk with their children about Christ. Demonstrate and discuss these concepts to the parents in your church. By raising the level of awareness with both parents and teachers, you will see children begin to ask questions and conversations will start. The beauty is seeing kids come to Christ and begin a wonderful spiritual journey with God.

Day 14: Questions

1) What are some of the reasons parents give for being nervous about talking to their children about Christ?

2) Which of these concepts would most help parents to feel comfortable talking to their children?

3) Based on what you have read today, how will you adapt your approach for talking to children about Christ?

DAY 15

Is Rotation Sunday School Okay?

Finding consistent teachers for Sunday school can become an overwhelming undertaking. Sometimes you are staring at ten classes that still need teachers. Other times it is that one last little spot that you need to fill to have a fully staffed Sunday school. I know the feeling. Then someone suggests rotation Sunday school and you wonder if that might be the perfect solution. Let's look into rotation Sunday school and see if it meets the objectives that we have for Sunday school.

The rotation method is used in Vacation Bible School and some midweek programs. Students enjoy a particular class for 20-30 minutes then move to the next class. This works great when your program has all morning or an extended time. Is it the best option for the children in Sunday School classes? I want to challenge you to be an advocate for the children. The relationships we build with kids are very important. These relationships can represent the relationship they can have with Christ. We offer acceptance, love, trust, and forgiveness just as Jesus offers to each of us. Our consistency of teaching the children reinforces our commitment to them and allows us to know them and disciple them.

Our kids need the same teachers greeting and teaching them when they arrive at Sunday school. This is especially important for the preschooler. Consistency in the classroom goes a long way towards making the child feel safe and secure. Many families are also visiting and looking for consistency in the teachers who care for their children. It is wonderful when a visiting child can be greeted by name at the door. Having the same teachers each week makes this possible. Children of all ages benefit from having the consistent expectations and schedule provided by having the same teachers in a room each week. Please consider at least one teacher that is always present and building relationships with the kids, even if you have to rotate other teachers through the class. Realize that rotation would not be the goal, but rather a temporary solution.

Another idea is to rotate kids to different classes. I know I enjoy the rotation plan on Wednesday nights and during VBS. There are two basic options within this idea. One, children rotate through different rooms/stations each week. The stations would most likely include a Bible story, an activity or craft, and an application or music time. This option is most like VBS rotations. The other option would be where a teacher only preps one lesson and teaches it for four weeks, each week to a different group. I observed a church using this model; the kids learned four parts of a single lesson (one part each week). This means the kids got twelve Bible stories that year. When a church offers 52 annual Bible story and learning times, there is a greater foundation for spiritual learning happening for the child. The main issue the rotation concept targets is minimizing the number of volunteers who are responsible for lesson preparation each week. With both options presented here, volunteers are still enlisted to lead each group to the different rooms or to assist the teacher with classroom management. As you consider this model of rotation Sunday school, consider the reasons from above and ask yourself the following questions: How are teachers effectively connecting to the lives of the kids? Are we wisely utilizing the time that we have with the children each week?

I suggest staying with the basic model of having two or more consistent teachers leading each class every week. Doing so will allow the volunteers to have great influence on each child's life, enabling them to spend more time loving the kids and leading them to Christ. Consistency with volunteers will be the greatest reward kids can have.

Day 15: Questions

1) What are the main reasons volunteers give for not wanting to teach each week?

2) Which reasons can you help alleviate through training and other assistance?

3) What are some specific steps you can take to enlist volunteers who are ready to teach, and to better equip your volunteers who are already serving?

DAY 16

The Extended Teaching Time Saga Continues

When I am struggling with filling spots for our extended teaching care time during the worship services, I often wonder, is it just me? Our program is set up with a volunteer rotation requiring them to serve about once every six weeks. It seems like my ministry gets a schedule finalized and printed just to get that call or text that someone wants to be removed. Ugh! It's enough to make a kids' minister run screaming for a place to hide. Do you have trouble finding enough volunteers during the worship service? If this has happened to you, then you know full well I'm not exaggerating. Of course, you use your sweet voice and ask if you can rearrange the schedule or place them in a different area to try and salvage them because empty lines with no names of workers already haunt you. Where is the easy button when you need it?

I have learned from a couple of past kids' ministers that they are not returning to the church ministry because of this issue. These aren't people who don't know ministry. They are seasoned ministers who are excellent in the classroom and leadership, but they are weary and worn with enlisting people who do not want to serve. I totally understand, but I am deeply saddened by the fact we are losing such great leaders in kids' ministry due to enlistment challenges.

I have attacked our program challenges head on. I have organized kids' ministry committees to lead in this challenge, and I have also hired wonderful women through the years only to find them quitting in tears. They believed in this ministry, but became defeated and heartbroken when they discovered that others did not care enough to volunteer. Often the expectation expressed by the church is that it is our job to make this magic happen—no excuses! My current coordinator has finally hit a wall, and the discouragement is overwhelming. Although my coordinator is giving it all she has, I need to step in and support her with more than saying, "We need helpers!"

As a kids' minister, what should you do when you have empty spaces and no one else to call? Here are some ideas to consider when you feel like your back is against the wall.

Pray

It's time to involve the prayer ministry, deacons, and individuals you know as intercessors. Let them know that a well-staffed program is a vital component of church health.

Teachers of adult classes

Plan some lunch meetings with teachers of adult classes to include them in helping to solve the shortage in volunteers. Contact the music minister and the choir too. Help them to see the need for providing quality instruction for children while their parents are participating in the worship service. In turn, the adult teachers can effectively communicate the need to their classes. Of course, use your friendly and tactful voice so as not to scare the teacher. No drama.

Pastor involvement

You may often feel that you don't want to go to the pastor unless it's a last resort. This is not right. You need his endorsement and leadership. He can speak about the need to minister to the youngest members of the congregation from the pulpit and possibly even in Sunday school classes. He has a vision for reaching young families. Let him speak it.

Staff planning

Set aside a focus time in your calendar for enlisting. This is a good time for positive publicity to be visual to the membership. When choosing the dates, stay away from summer months, holidays, or other times when you might be competing for attention. Involve the entire church staff so they can support the push and not trump you by introducing a different ministry focus. Explain your vision up front so the dates are protected.

Positive publicity includes:
- Video recording the experience for an announcement.
- Posting photos and words of appreciation from parents.
- Asking the pastor to serve one Sunday as an example.

Clear Expectations and Mission

Clearly explain the mission and goal of this extended teaching time. Offer training and classroom support with pre-organized activities to be used. You might have a college professor who is willing to serve, but who is completely untrained in what to do with a room full of two-year-olds. Help him or her get acclimated so they feel successful and not a failure.

Transitions

Instruct teachers to do well at transitioning over to volunteers after Sunday school. Have them share what is going on and any activities the kids have enjoyed. It will give the volunteer the handle they need to get started. A great way for the Sunday school teacher to encourage the volunteers is to have the teacher hand out thank you cards to the volunteers. Sometimes you forget that little things can make a difference: send cards and texts yourself acknowledging others builds friendship.

Do not grow weary in well doing (see Galatians 6:9). When your sacrifice costs something, presenting it to the Lord is so sweet.

Day 16: Questions

1) Write out all the ways that extended teaching time specifically benefits your church so that you can share your thoughts with others.

2) What is most frustrating to you when staffing your extending teaching program?

3) Which one of these suggestions best addresses your frustration? Write a step action for putting it into practice at your church.

DAY 17

Teaching Children? Remember This!

Preparing to teach children can quickly seem like an overwhelming task with several different components that you want to incorporate in your teaching session. You may often feel like a drill sergeant is rattling off a litany of things for you to remember. You can get so caught up in one particular aspect of your presentation that you can forget what you are really there to do. Your main goal is to present biblical principles and stories so that the children will eventually come to a personal relationship with Christ. Take a deep breath. Here are some key points to keep you on track when teaching children:

Key #1—Apply these principles

- Learning should be fun. Learning should be fun for you and the children. If you aren't excited and sharing that enthusiasm with children, they aren't going to be excited either. Think about ways to make the topic meaningful by using fun activities.

- Target the age level of the children. If you are teaching preschoolers, don't give an abstract illustration or expect them to finish a ten-piece puzzle in 30 seconds flat. Use appropriate, real-life examples to tie in the Bible story for elementary age children. Nothing will tank your lesson faster than presenting material that is over or under your audience's age level.

- We must "do" in order to "learn." For children, having fun includes having something to do. Children learn through play and actively participating. Incorporate hands-on activities, relevant games, and times where they can put into practice what they have learned. Consider having them help pack sacks for the food pantry when you are talking about being a servant.

Key #2—Know your audience

- Children can think and reason; therefore, they can draw conclusions. Don't underestimate their ability to draw conclusions and come to an appropriate deduction.

- Preschoolers and younger elementary children don't understand symbolism yet. Talking about Jesus coming into their heart or Jesus knocking on their heart's door will only lead to confusion. Use concrete terminology and the kids will walk away understanding what was presented.

- Children like heroes. These heroes can be incorporated into the message as biblical examples. Be careful not to mix imaginary characters with real characters from the Bible.

- Remove distractions if possible. If something can be a distraction, it will become one for children. Sometimes it can be difficult to identify everything that is a potential distraction, but removing the obvious ones is a great place to start.

- The attention span of a child is about one minute per year of age. Think about it. This means the attention span of a nine-year-old is nine minutes. Remember to change up activities; don't have children sit and listen to someone talk for the entire hour. Incorporate a game, a discussion, or re-enactment of the story. You don't have to change the message you are trying to convey, but you do need to consider the different learning approaches and how your delivery method can reach out to each child.

Key #3—Remember the following:

- Use appropriate words and body language.

- Think about the image you want to convey. (Smile and look friendly.)

- Make eye contact. (Making eye contact means making a connection.)

- Always find ways to let the kids participate.

- You learn best when you are engaged in the activity and enjoying it yourself.

Day 17: Questions

1) Which one of these keys is easiest for you to put into practice this week? Why do you think this is?

2) Which one of these keys is most out of your comfort zone? Why do you think this is?

3) What is one thing you can do to incorporate this particular tip into your next session?

DAY 18

Bible Teaching Checklist

Ensuring that your teachers are prepared and ready for their teaching hour is one of the most foundational tasks of children's ministry. Here's a quick checklist for your teachers to help make their hour meaningful and productive.

- Teachers plan activities that naturally lead to talking about Bible truths.

- Teachers talk about the Bible as the children are involved in activities.

- Teachers plan a variety of activities for the children to choose so that each child can learn in the way God has gifted him or her to learn.

- Teachers use Bible verses and phrases, Bible story conversation, and songs to encourage Bible learning on the child's level of understanding.

- Teachers place Bibles in Bible learning centers for children to touch and use.

- Teachers listen as children talk.

- Teachers are prepared to begin teaching when the first child arrives.

- Teachers build relationships with children and parents by committing to teach every week.

- Teachers are trained to use the curriculum and are equipped with an understanding of the importance of Bible teaching.

- Teachers wash hands after changing a diaper, after assisting a child with toileting, after wiping a child's nose or mouth, before feeding a baby or serving snacks, and before and after administering first aid.

Sanitizing the Classroom

- Bleach solution can be used to disinfect toys, furnishings, hands, and other items.

- Mix 1/4 cup of bleach with one gallon of water (or 1 tablespoon bleach to 1 quart water).

- Prepare fresh solution for each teaching time.

Note: If you choose to spray down cribs with the bleach solution, make sure you store the solution in solid colored (not opaque) spray bottles because light breaks down bleach.

This checklist can seem daunting at first, but tackling just a couple of items at a time can make a marked difference in the overall experience of both the teachers and the children in your ministry.

Day 18: Questions

1) Name three things from this checklist that you and your teachers already do well.

2) What are three items that could improve?

3) What are specific tasks that you can do to help teachers be successful in these three areas of improvement?

DAY 19

Should Sixth Grade Be in Youth Ministry?

Many churches are currently debating whether sixth graders should be in the youth group or the children's ministry. Because of the rise in middle schools that include sixth through eighth grade, a lot of churches have chosen to include the sixth grade in their youth ministry. Is this decision what is best for the sixth graders or just what is most convenient for the church?

Moving sixth graders into youth ministry is a mistake, especially if the youth ministry includes sixth grade all the way through twelfth grade. These ministries typically experience one of two scenarios. Either the ministry will have mostly middle school kids because high school students don't want to babysit, or mostly high school students because the younger students are intimidated and wide-eyed about the conversations and actions of high school students. The span in age is extensive considering the physical changes, responsibilities, and independence of the older group.

Some churches have realized the gap is too large and have created a six through eighth grade middle school ministry with their own youth minister who is totally dedicated to their spiritual development. While this is a much better option than a combined middle school and high school ministry, it still isn't the best option for sixth graders who are very much in a transition stage of life.

The best-case scenario is to create a transitional preteen ministry for sixth grade and possibly even seventh grade. While the kids might feel too old for children's ministry, they need a transition step before youth or student ministry. This successfully occurred at a previous church of mine. The ministry ran 40-45 kids each Wednesday night. The curriculum opened the door to youth topics, content, and Bible application but it didn't dive too deep. We delved just deep enough to explain what the adolescent subject matter is about and the Bible had the answers they were searching for.

This preteen ministry had its own events, camp, classes, and choir. Every event was customized, and it really paid off. The ministry had theme nights, fun events, and parent interaction through the parents leading in groups during the teaching times. The theme for the ministry was 1 Timothy 4:12: *Let no one despise your youth; instead, you should be an example to the believers in speech, in conduct, in love, in faith, in purity.* This truth was woven throughout our entire ministry. The preteen ministry team was purposeful and repeated the same curriculum every two years since kids cycled through in that time period. Parents were thankful and attendance was terrific. Kids often said they didn't want to promote up into the youth.

Having a separate sixth and seventh grade ministry also blessed the children's ministry because the younger kids were so excited about getting to the preteen ministry. Children were able to look forward to an exciting new division while still being able to benefit from age-appropriate teaching and interactions.

Day 19: Questions

1) What are some of the misconceptions that you face when it comes to sixth graders and the youth ministry?

2) Make a pro and con list regarding the creation of a separate preteen ministry at your church.

3) What are some specific steps that you can take to provide for the needs of the sixth graders at your church?

DAY 20
Enlisting Men to Teach Kids

Enlist a man to teach for each class of preschool and children. Men are often few and far between in the childhood ministries department, but they are such an integral part of your ministry. Why? Men offer a positive Christian role model that many children are lacking. With many children coming from single-parent homes, the need for a positive male role model is greater than ever. Department directors often say that the mere presence of a man helps in guiding behavior. For the children who have Christian men in their life, having a man teach in the classroom will only reinforce building spiritual foundations and relationships that enable kids to trust Jesus.

Here are a few characteristics of men to consider when enlisting:

Men Enjoy a Challenge
Activity without engagement leads to burnout. When you are enlisting teachers, explain the routine and uniqueness of teaching in a children's classroom. This will allow men to be able to correctly engage in the teaching process.

Men Want to Know They Make a Difference

There are definitely tangible rewards like a hug, a smile, and "I love you, Mr. Mark." Be sure to communicate the positive impact the man is making in the classroom and with the children. Men are more likely to invite others to come and see what is happening.

Men Will Accept Responsibility

As you recruit teachers, clearly communicate the responsibilities and expectations. Don't dumb it down. This allows you the opportunity to explain how to teach preschoolers or children and answer questions to clarify any confusion or misunderstanding.

Men Prefer to Hear Feedback

Coaching your teachers, especially men, will reinforce correct teaching to the children in your ministry. Be cautious not to come across as demeaning or overbearing. Don't forget to focus on the positive. Men know they are making a positive contribution when they receive recognition.

Men Explore Risk Taking

Men will take risks in order to explore their talents. Allowing men to be responsible for certain tasks will give ownership to the teaching process. Assigning special tasks such as group time activities, greeting the children, or telling the Bible story will allow men to explore new challenges. Respond with feedback anytime a teacher takes a risk outside his routine responsibilities.

Men Need to Feel Valued

When men feel they are valued, they will most often reciprocate that feeling. Let your teachers know you appreciate their commitment to teaching preschoolers and children. Communicate what a positive difference they make.

Men Will be Advocates for the Future

Talk about your hopes and dreams. Deacons and other men in leadership who teach in the children's ministry department will become advocates for the needs of preschoolers and children when considering budgets, buildings, and ministry needs.

Men who have served in preschool and children's classrooms for years said they were tremendously grateful that someone asked them to teach. You could bless the life of a man deeply by inviting him to teach kids.

Day 20: Questions

1) What is your biggest hurdle you face when asking men to teach?

2) What are three things you can do to make working in childhood ministry more appealing and accessible to men?

3) Write a list of five men to prayerfully pursue for positions within your ministry.

DAY 21

How Welcoming Is Your Children's Ministry?

It is often a good idea to take a step back and evaluate your ministry through the lens of someone who is visiting your church. Volunteers, teachers, and staff can all become focused on getting their specific tasks done or just get a little stuck in the rut of "This is how our ministry has always looked." Taking the time to look through the eyes of a visitor often helps us know where our ministry needs to adapt and where our ministry is excelling. Here is a brief survey of ten measurements to consider as you assess your ministry:

1. Greeters know how to lead guests to our children's ministry area.

2. The children's ministry area is easy to find.

3. Childhood greeters are energetic and knowledgeable— enthusiastically helping children and their families find the right places to be.

4. Children's rooms are clean and fresh.

5. Children's rooms are inviting and safe.

6. Children's teachers arrive early and are willing to stay late.

7. Children's teachers actively teach children.

8. Children's teachers contact children and their families during the week.

9. Our pastor and other leaders take time to be with children.

10. Our church realizes the importance of the children's ministry.

Day 21: Questions

1) What area is your ministry excelling at? Why do you think your church is doing so well at this?

2) What area is your ministry struggling with? What are three steps that you can take to improve this area?

3) Which areas are in the middle of the road? How can you step it up a notch to make those areas ones that your ministry is outstanding?

DAY 22

When a Child Dies

Having a child within your ministry pass away is unthinkable, but at some point during your ministry you will face this. I know, because it has happened to me. My wife and I had been praying non-stop for a particular child's healing. Each night as we read the posts on Facebook from his daddy, our hearts hurt for this precious family. The family and everyone who knew them experienced a roller-coaster of emotions. There was great hope and encouragement, then a fever and disappointment. More treatments ushered in more hope, followed by no success. The church rallied together, calling on hundreds of people who boldly joined the fight by praying and giving, but there was no successful treatment. The parents were exhausted and didn't even know it. The fight for healing was very long, but they never gave up hope. The doctors tried everything and then came the news that there was nothing more they could do. We prayed and cried and prayed some more. The child died and was free from pain and alive in the arms of Jesus. Today we celebrate the life of this seven-year-old boy and lean on our Lord even more.

As children's ministers and teachers, how are you going to minister? You don't want to plan for these life events because you don't want them to happen. The problem is, death happens and you may not be prepared. Just like me, I suppose you will sit down and cry (maybe daily). Good. After you dry your tears and wipe the snot off your face, like I did, it is time to get organized. This is a critical time in your ministry for you to reach out to the family that is desperately hurting. You will find joy in ministering to them during their time of grief.

Here are some ways you can minister to a family that is dealing with the death of a child:

1. Pray for the family. Pray for the immediate family, the extended family, and others who were closely associated with the child. Pray for peace, acceptance, understanding, and the strength to face each day.

2. Offer to watch young children during the funeral service and to watch the house while they are away. Offering childcare while making funeral arrangements is appreciated too.

3. Plan a meal after the funeral. This is such a needed time for the extended family to be together and lean on each other for support.

4. Arrange meals to be provided for the family in the weeks following the funeral. The family will most likely be going through the motions for a period of time after the death. Taking care of this physical need will be a great blessing.

5. Make a scrapbook for the parents. Include pictures and thoughts from friends in the church and community.

Ask others to write about things they remember or loved most about the child. Be sure to include teachers from school and classmates.

6. Set an anniversary reminder on your calendar for the next ten years. This way you can reach out in love with a note or text each year because you remembered. There is an incredible, healing power that comes when you show that you remember their grief and are continuing to support them.

7. Send occasional texts of Bible verses and reminders of your prayers for them. Reaching out to the family in the weeks and the months after the funeral is something that tends to be forgotten. Show them that you are still grieving with them.

8. Offer times to go get coffee and talk. Be a listener and cry if needed. Be real. Be cautious about offering empty platitudes or quick, simplified answers.

9. Never underestimate a hug and whisper, with an "I'm still praying." Your care is deeply appreciated.

Here are a few things not to say or do when someone loses a child.
- Don't minimize their loss by saying things such as "God will give you other children" and "At least you have other children." One child's life will never replace another child's life.

- Don't tell them you know how they feel. Every situation

is different and everyone handles loss differently. You can say you are sorry they are hurting, but don't assume you know exactly what they are going through.

- Don't tell them Christian platitudes such as "God will never give you more than you can bear." Also, giving pat answers generally doesn't help the situation.

- Don't stop and talk to them about their loss when they are preoccupied with a task or in a crowd. Be aware of your surroundings. You want to respect their feelings and boundaries.

Day 22: Questions

1) What intimidates you the most when you think about dealing with a family who has lost a child?

2) What is one other idea that you could add to the list?

3) What are some verses that you could use that would be a comfort to the family? (Example: Nahum 1:7)

DAY 23

We Need Help with Enlistment!

One of the most time-consuming and energy-zapping tasks you face as a children's ministry leader is enlisting and retaining volunteers. You lead an army of volunteers in children's ministry. While it will often be an overwhelming task, there are appropriate steps that you can take to lay the foundation for a well-staffed volunteer program. Here are four tips to remember:

Pray

Surely you knew I was going to say this. It's true though, I pray a lot. I also remind myself, this is God's church and He fits the body together perfectly (see Romans 12:3-8). No need for worry. It's an ongoing process and takes time. As soon as all the positions are filled, someone will need to quit or we will grow and need another class. Growth is a good thing in case you forgot.

Find a Balance Between the Emergency, the Urgent, and the Ideal

The *emergency* is Saturday night and no teacher for tomorrow morning.

Who is on the bench that I can call to sub? I put together a list of people who are willing to serve on the bench by going to all the adult classes and asking them to serve in that specific role. My starters are in the game, but I need people on the bench to join the game in progress sometimes. Don't call the bench people every week. Spread the love. Some prefer babies; others prefer elementary age kids. Then there are adults who are parents or grandparents; they aren't scared of any age and can work anywhere. Create an extra stash of curriculum or email them lesson packets so they have some ideas to use in the classroom. Don't send volunteers into the game empty-handed; we don't want to waste valuable teaching opportunities with kids. Giving them a game plan will help them have a more successful experience in the classroom.

The *urgent* are those open positions that are a constant part of growth or change. The need exists on an ongoing basis and you are actively seeking to enlist a volunteer for the classroom.

The *ideal* is the plan that we are striving for, when each volunteer is in the perfect position to use their God-given talents, and every open spot is filled. While we should always be working toward the ideal, we also must realize that God is often teaching and stretching us during the emergency and the urgent.

Enlistment Is a Slow Cooker, Not a Drive-Thru Window

It would be great if we could just order a teacher and drive away with an expert, but finding a teacher often requires asking, praying, and asking again. A good course to follow is asking the potential volunteer to come and watch. The next step is enlisting the volunteer in a helper role, and then later as regular volunteer who you can begin training and encouraging. I can almost hear you saying, "How am I supposed to be that patient when Sunday keeps coming around each week?" Let me remind you again, God is working everywhere. He may bring you a teacher that someone else trained and developed, and now you get the harvest. He may be working with someone to take steps of faith in this role and they are trying to trust God.

While you are asking others, waiting on the Lord, and watching the calendar move forward, build in a detour. I have driven past our city's construction on I-40 for four years. When they said it would take four years, I thought that was forever. "Don't they know we need that road now?" Four years later it finally opened. The new road is great! The detours and traffic jams were awful but the inconvenience was worth it. The same principle applies to volunteer enlistment. Here's what I practice and suggest to you: find a volunteer that can work for a month. That's all. After the month, thank them and let them go. Keep your promises and don't beg. I have begged and it is never flattering. You can set up a couple of months ahead and give yourself a little breathing room. This is not ideal for the children, but it is the reality for now.

Take No for an Answer

The Bible says in James 5:12, *"Let your yes be 'yes' and your no, 'no'."* I might not want to hear people tell me no; however, I would rather they be honest with me than quit a few weeks later or just not show up some Sunday (both of which have happened to me). Be gracious and accepting when told no, just like you are when you hear yes and the angels sing in Heaven.

Maybe some of my practices will help you to think through a strategy and move out of the wilderness of frustration. Start in the prayer closet and then begin drawing up plans for a detour path that moves you a little farther forward and gives you some breathing room so that you can think more clearly. Building this road takes time, but the new highway will be such a reward.

Day 23: Questions

1) What are your initial feelings when thinking about enlisting a new volunteer?

2) Which one of these tips do you most need to work on when enlisting volunteers? What can you personally do to make progress in this area?

3) Take a few moments to jot down your current needs. While your ultimate goal is always the ideal volunteer, which needs could be filled with a "detour" volunteer?

DAY 24
Kindergarten vs. First Grade

When to Transition to the Children's Division

Many churches want to move kindergarten classes out of the preschool division and into the children's division. Maybe the decision has to do with space constraints. Maybe it involves children's worship, curriculum choices, or any number of reasons. I was lured into this way of thinking too. But wait! Here's what I learned when looking into the details of the decision.

Let's look at a comparison list of kindergarteners versus first graders to fully see the differences between the two grades.

Characteristics of Kindergarteners
- Need active play and like to move freely during games and music
- Refine physical gains made during the first four years
- Girls may display more maturity at this age than boys
- Begin to separate fact from fantasy

- Can follow simple instructions in doing tasks
- Remember and like to tell Bible stories
- Can use the Bible and like to find Bible phrases located by Bible markers
- Recognize church as a special place where people learn about God and Jesus
- Are developing a conscience and may experience guilt for misbehavior
- Cooperate in play with peers
- Show limited ability to share
- Exclude peers when angry rather than using name calling
- Display a full range of emotions
- Are prone to self-criticism and guilt

Characteristics of First Graders

- Are less self-centered than earlier years
- Continue developing a conscience
- Are forming concepts of personal worth
- Can put many Bible teachings into practice
- Are active learners
- Have surface-level emotions (easy tears or laughter)
- Enjoy informal play without many rules
- Show their feelings in behavior rather than words
- Are concrete thinkers who do not understand symbolic language
- Have limited reading skills

Although most kindergarteners are attending all-day school now, their brains are still learning with early childhood methods. Their classroom experience revolves around activity centers for hands-on, experiential learning through play and group time. Probably the most intensive work kindergarteners do is learning to follow instructions, respect the teacher and other classmates, work together, walk in line, raise a hand before speaking, and take turns. The main focus is on social courtesies and operating within a group. While many people think a child already knows how to interact in an educational and social setting when they go to school, it is simply not true. The teachers work hard to teach and practice these skills with our children daily.

If a child advances to the children's division before learning these skills, there is chaos. Teachers become frustrated because we have set both the teachers and the kindergarteners up to struggle. Older children who the kindergarteners have been mixed with are frustrated too. Do yourself a favor and allow kindergarteners to be early childhood learners, experiencing new challenges such as introducing longer group times, practicing social courtesies, applying Bible truths to scenarios you introduce, laying foundations for salvation, and opportunities for service. Celebrate the way that God has designed kindergarteners to learn and grow.

Day 24: Questions

1) How can you help your leadership team (teachers, volunteers, etc.) get on board with keeping kindergarten in the preschool division?

2) What are some of the reasons that people give you for including kindergarten in the children's division?

3) What are three immediate benefits to your particular program when you choose to keep kindergarteners in the preschool division?

DAY 25:

Five Simple Steps to Sharing a Classroom

While I was the lead teacher of two-year-olds' preschool, I was frustrated with the roommates who shared my classroom. Our church had a weekday ministry, so the classroom was used six out seven days a week. The equipment and toys in the classroom were heavily used. I noticed the classroom and toys were not being cleaned, and brown grunge was building up. I mentioned it to the minister, but no action was being taken. All of the weekday ministry's drawers and cabinet doors were padlocked so that we could not use any of their supplies. I found myself setting the dirty toys in the hall, bathroom, and high cabinets. I turned bookshelves around to the wall so those items were not available to the kids. I brought the needed items from the resource room and my home. It was a lot of trouble, but it worth it to me since my roommates were so difficult to work with.

Most churches have to share space, either with other ministries or with other programs within your ministry. Sharing space can often become quite the sticky situation. Can I share something with you though? Sharing space is a *mindset*. Decide today to share with others.

Realize that each preschool and children's class or program is there for the same purpose: to lay spiritual foundations in the lives of young children. Recognize that you are a team working together to provide what is best for children.

1. Get to know the team. Plan a meeting with everyone who shares the room. Talk about schedules and activities of each ministry. Ask other teachers, "What can I do to help you?" Pray for each teacher and ministry sharing the room.

2. Make a plan. Standard preschool and children's equipment remains in the classroom. Work together during the meeting to arrange the furniture in a way that benefits all children and ministries. Make a diagram of the room arrangement and post in the classroom. Plan to leave the furniture the same from week to week.

3. Treat others the way you want to be treated. How do you feel when you find the classroom is a disaster? Determine to *always* leave the classroom the way you want to find it. Put toys away, restock supplies, and generally leave the room nicer than when you came in.

4. Bring in unit- or topic-specific toys and materials during each session, and return the toys to the resource room when the class is finished.

5. Be the leader and set the tone. We want children to share, so let's role model. Throw away locks and labels. Be the leader in your ministry who refuses to talk about others, forgives when someone leaves a mess, and determines to share with a good attitude.

Day 25: Questions

1) What do you think is your biggest stumbling block to teachers joyfully sharing classrooms?

2) In which one of these five steps do your teachers and volunteers already excel? Take the time to encourage them in their efforts every chance you can.

3) Evaluate your ministry. What can you as a leader do to model these five steps to your volunteers?

DAY 26

Storytelling

Storytelling is an engaging tool for children's ministry. Children never tire of hearing Bible stories, just as they love frequently reading a favorite book over again. As a children's minister, learning to open the Bible and tell the story in your own words is an invaluable skill. Being able to capture your children's attention and make the story relevant to their lives never gets old.

Consider these tips to enhance your storytelling:

1. Know the story well. Learn what the story is emphasizing and the purpose of the story.

2. Consider the age of the children and adjust your vocabulary. Explain words and help children practice pronouncing Bible names for better learning and retention.

3. Notice what senses are used in the story and highlight them (the smell of rain, the feel of hot sand, the sounds of animals, or the sight of a clear blue sky).

4. Sequence the events in the story in your mind. Memorize the beginning and the end of the story. Utilize the sequencing the events to tell the middle of the story in your own words. A simple note page in your Bible will assist you.

5. Eliminate any elements that are not necessary in the story.

6. Practice telling the story so that you are comfortable with it. By practicing the story, you can change words and try inflections with your voice to give you greater confidence.

7. Catch the children's attention at the beginning with your voice. Use action words, facial expressions, and eye contact to keep their attention. Lower your voice to draw them into the story.

8. Save the props and pictures for after you have told the story for the first time. After the story, show the picture or props to reinforce and review the story.

9. Use a Bible that is open to the story passage while you tell the story. This will help children know the story came from the Bible and is a truth from God. Encourage children to use their Bibles by providing time to locate the verses. Practice Bible skills during this time. Say the phrase, "The Bible says..." so children know this story is from the Bible.

10. Enthusiasm is necessary. Use inflections. Whisper to get their attention, but avoid screaming and shouting so kids are not frightened.

Remember monotone is *boring*.

Day 26: Questions

1) Choose a favorite Bible story to practice storytelling. Why is this particular story so relevant to you?

2) How can you use these reasons to help you as you tell the story?

3) What are three specific things you can add to the story to draw children in (specific senses, emotions, etc.)?

DAY 27

When Kids Become Wild Monkeys

Classroom management can be an overwhelming undertaking, especially when you feel like you are wrangling wild monkeys. Let's look at a possible scenario for teachers who work with three-year-olds, four-year-olds, kindergarten, first grade, and second grade. Most teachers who work with kids in this age group would agree there should be a lot of movement in classes filled with these age groups. However, my teacher friend found that when she was in charge of a class that's immediately following a class where children sit for pretty much the whole time, her class often acted like a group of wild monkeys. There are too many wiggles and no good productive way to get them out – even given her plan for lots of movement. This particular teacher was beginning to feel like she was at her wit's end.

As a minister, how do you help this teacher? Start by reassuring her that her class activities sound like lots of fun. Gently remind her that sometimes the personalities of a class causes less success with one group compared to another. The first mistake teachers often make is thinking all kids are the same, or that every class should respond in a specific way. Realize that every person, young or old, desires and feels most comfortable with a specific learning approach. The learning approaches are: visual, auditory, hands-on, reflective, relational, physical, nature, and musical. As teachers, try to identify which best appeals to each child and begin providing those activities.

With the free movement design and no assigned activities this teacher enjoyed in her classroom, although it might only take a couple of children to cause it to unravel. Instruct the teacher to look and see if any of the kids might be an instigator of wild monkey behavior. If so, help him or her to assign special leadership roles for the child to assist the teacher. This will allow the teacher more time with the child to work together and have a conversation before the class gets involved in an activity. Remind the teacher to use words of affirmation and appreciation with the child. This might help the child to focus and self-regulate his or her actions. When the child wanders into forbidden territory of behavior, be quick to go to the child, hold his or her hands and speak directly, eye to eye, about their choices. No shouting across the room or hinting. Be clear and in the child's face. A terrific and positive way to begin the class is to ask the children entering the classroom to sit for about five minutes in the group circle before moving around for the rest of the hour. The teacher can have quiet conversations and help the children get ready for learning.

Building a relationship with the child is always going to benefit the teacher and the child. Have the teacher visit at the child's home. Encourage the teacher to take a small gift or photos of the child from the classroom. Let the child see the teacher interact with his or her parents. Remember to tell the child, "I'm so glad you're in my class." Doing so will help the child to feel valued and accepted in the class. A child who understands he or she is valued by the teacher will begin to behave better.

Finally, let me suggest using large motor skills (large muscle groups) by incorporating marching, twirling ribbons, relay races, and other gross motor activities to focus attention on the teacher as a large group activity at the beginning of the class. This will allow the teacher to establish leadership, burn off wiggle energy, and provide the opportunity for the children to enjoy one another before working in small group activities. Get involved in the activities with the children and laugh with the kids. My class is always drawn to me when I laugh and enjoy them.

Day 27: Questions

1) What is a common misconception that you encounter when trying to help teachers realize that each child learns differently and that the combination of children in a specific class might necessitate an adjustment in teaching practices?

2) Which learning approach is hardest for you to relate to and teach to?

3) What are three large muscle activities that you could suggest for children as they begin the teaching time? Keep these in my mind to suggest in moments of crisis.

DAY 28

Partnering with Parents

P Pray for Them.

They have a huge job entrusted to them to raise their children to serve and love God. Pray continually for them as you support and equip them for this task (see Philippians 1:3-5).

A Accept Their Child.

Do not compare their child with another child. Know what is unique about their child. Be excited when you see their child. They are watching to see your reaction. Do you have a genuine smile or your face, a half-hearted greeting, or a look of dread?

R Reach Out to Them.

Find out what is happening in their lives. Find out what their family life is like. When a ministry opportunity arises, go for it. Organize ministry for the family in times of family change—birth, death, sickness, loss of job, deployment, etc. When everything seems to return to normal, continue to check on the family.

T Take a Walk in Their Shoes.

Think about their day. Be ready to accept their child as soon as they get there. Know when they are returning so that you can have their child ready to go without delay.

N Notify Them of *Real* Issues.

Notice the emphasis on the word *real*—notify of character flaws, excessive aggressiveness, and when other children are injured. Make sure you are focusing on actions beyond typical childlike behavior. Don't tell the parent of a two year old that he or she is still having problems sharing the box of crayons with friends. This is a skill that most two year olds are still trying to master. Nothing erodes the relationship with a parent like being told their child is having problems every time they pick them up from their classroom.

E Encourage Them.

Be aware of how you react to a parent. Your reaction could be the breaking point for a parent or the saving hand reaching out in the middle of the storm. Help these parents get through life by being a source of encouragement.

R Recognize Them and Their Family.

Calling someone by name allows them to know that you care specifically for them. Know the child's name. Know the parents' first names and say them. Know the rest of the family—other children, live-in family members. Praying regularly for them will help you to better recall the names of the family members.

Be intentional in your actions and attitudes during moments with parents. We create most of our problems by the way we act and treat others. If you purposefully partner with parents, you set up an environment that builds relationships to effectively impact the next generation by demonstrating God's love.

Day 28: Questions

1) Think of a family in your ministry that has been hard to partner with. What makes it hard to partner with them?

2) What are some specific ways that you can chose to reach out to them and partner with them?

3) Begin a prayer list and log dates of conversation so each family is included.

DAY 29

When Teachers Don't Attend Worship

I have a unique situation. We have four morning worship services and our pastor preaches all four services. We also have two Sunday school hours where I have terrific preschool teachers who choose to teach the first hour, and then attend the parents of preschoolers Sunday school class where I teach about 35 parents. It's a great community of sharp, growing Christian parents whom I love sharing life with weekly.

Since our pastor preaches two of the services within the same worship hour, parents have one option and that is the early service. I'm not going to lie. It is the least appealing service for my teachers. The crowd is much older in age, the music is strongly traditional, and the hour is early for young parents. Most will not attend Sunday night. Watching the recorded service on the web is not the same as attending. I feel like these nine teachers will burn out soon since they are not experiencing corporate worship. Even if they teach all year, there is no staying power. They are running on empty with a feeling that they are being cheated while others are experiencing something terrific. This feeling is absolutely true.

When I talked to each one about my concern, I learned I was correct. Missing worship was getting old. Only a couple of teachers were trying to attend on Sunday night to have corporate worship. I made the suggestion that I would like to provide an early class for their kids where I would have some preschool Sunday school activities prepared and provide breakfast for one month. They could come a bit early to slip into the service during the last hymn and listen to the sermon. They were pleasantly surprised. We began the next Sunday and I was looking forward to it. Two reasons: first, I enjoy teaching preschool and these kids are really terrific. Second, my wonderful teachers get to be fed and included in worship.

I know I'm adding another thing to my list, but it feels right to serve these servants. I hope it will meet the need and become something we provide weekly so that our teachers can have staying power. The nine teachers would be very hard to replace.

I know my situation is probably little different from how your church is set up. But I believe all volunteers struggle with this issue at some point. Volunteers serve during one hour and want to be a part of a small group during the second worship service hour. Sometimes the teacher just doesn't see the value in attending corporate worship, and would rather serve in the preschool department both hours. Occasionally, a teacher just wants to serve on Sunday and leaves directly afterward because they just don't see the value in attending "big church." Whatever the scenario, one thing is constant: volunteers and teachers alike need the time of corporate worship. They need to be refueled by hearing the Word of God spoken to them. They need the time to respond to Him with singing, prayer, and meditation. They need to be a part of the church as a whole, and see how God is working within the lives of the entire church body. Bottom line: corporate worship is a necessity for the spiritual health of all believers, and occasionally our volunteers need us to help them make it a priority.

Day 29: Questions

1) Do your teachers know that attending corporate worship is something you value and expect of them? If not, what can you do to promote the need for corporate worship?

2) What reasons have your teachers given for not attending corporate worship?

3) What have you done to meet your teachers' needs? Are there ways that you can assist them so that attending corporate worship is easier?

DAY 30

You are Making a Difference

This story reminds me of the importance of leading children to Christ, and the short time we are given with them. Deuteronomy 6 instructs us to impress these biblical truths on our kids. Making impressions on children happens anytime they are around you. Here is a good example how God taught me the value of my time with children: I picked up Nathan and Nolan for Bible drill on Wednesdays. These twin boys were quick to tell me that they enjoyed going to the church, and also that their dad was in jail. Probably more information than I needed but it didn't change my mind about these two boys. I was glad to give them a ride to church, and our conversations were usually interesting to say the least.

They were new to the church scene, so we practiced our verses during our drive each Wednesday. I gave them both Bibles, and we talked about different stories each week as we rode together. My theologian third grade daughter often began the stories, and I jumped in to make the needed corrections as she explained the Bible. One day Nathan asked, "Who is God?" I explained how God is our creator and He loves us. He quickly came back with, "I know He don't like me." I surprised Nathan when I agreed, and then said, "God *loves* you Nathan." Everyone was quiet as I continued to explain why and how. Our conversation was halted when we arrived at church to begin all the great fun for the evening. Although I was unable to explain everything in our limited time, I knew it was enough for them to begin processing, and we could talk more as we ride together each week.

I began to pray for these two neighbor boys. The next day Nathan brought his leftover sandwich from his lunch that day and knocked on our door. My daughter opened the door and Nathan handed her the sandwich with these words, "Give this to your dad, he's the best dad I know." I'm convinced that my relationship with Nathan had opened a door. Truth is caught more than taught. When Christmas break was over and our Bible drill class started up again, I asked my daughter if Nathan and Nicholas were riding to church with us again. She called and heard the bad news, "They moved. Their mom broke up with her boyfriend."

When she told me the news, I went to my bedroom and sat down and began to ponder. I will never see those boys again. I hope my limited time (actions and words) with them planted truth that will not be easily forgotten. I pray there will be other good Christian influences in their lives that will continue to build on the seed of the gospel that was planted. I continue to view my ministry with children as brief. They are not with us forever. They must be prepared for what is coming next.

Day 30: Questions

1) Do you operate your ministry from a heart of childcare or of discipling for Christ?

2) Create a prayer list for kids to accept Christ. Begin praying each day.

3) Create a regular discussion with teachers where you contribute and learn about the needs of children so that your team is more unified when impressing these Bible truths on kids.

DAY 31

The Hidden Blessings of Plan B

Plan B never seems as good as plan A. A few summers ago, I was staring square at plan B. Rain in Oklahoma is always a great thing, unless it is camp activity time. When the thunder rolls, the activities don't go as planned. On this particular day, the children could not go out to the ropes course to climb the rock wall or ride the zip line. No one could enjoy the waterfront canoes and pedal boats because of the danger of lightning. Two hundred sets of eyes were looking at me with the question, "What are we gonna *do*?" written all over their faces.

My first thought was, we should all go back to bed and get some much-needed sleep. While I knew the sponsors would love the extra sleep, my idea was not going to fly with the children. I began to explain the rainy day plan. Plan B was met with dissatisfied faces from both the children and the sponsors, but we had to make the best of it. After I explained to the sponsors that the alternative was to go to your cabin and try to wrangle wild monkeys, they became very cooperative. While the day didn't quite turn out as planned, the sponsors and campers were able to spend some quality time just getting to know each other, and some really great friendships were forged despite the change in plans.

The disappointment of the campers and the momentary panic of the sponsors at the change of plans is how you may feel when a teacher calls on Wednesday an hour before class begins to let you know he or she won't be coming. You try to respond with grace, but your emotions are a little too obvious. Substitute teachers on Wednesday night, or any other time, are not easily found. Even if you can find substitutes, you know plan B will not be as exciting as the usual terrific lessons taught in the class. You might even have to step in yourself and try to make the best of it.

Recently I filled in for a missing teacher and had to muster a smile on my way to the classroom. I walked in and found a new teacher who was already frazzled. I was not acquainted with all the kids, but I got right to work. When it was time to dismiss, I realized the blessings I had received. I had a new teacher who watched me model how to lead the class and was now more prepared for the job. I also enjoyed meeting new kids and getting to know them better. That does not happen in the hall as the kids and their parents are leaving the building. I began a friendship with children that day, which would not have happened otherwise.

My blessings far outweighed my challenges that day. I was on edge, but God had a plan and I am glad I was included. My ministry was better for it. Our blessings can come out of our challenges if we allow God to use them for His glory.

As you prepare for events in your ministry, it is best to have a plan B already in place in case you need it. Think about potential issues that you might encounter while at camp, and then have options, such as a rainy day box full of activities, ready to go. Have a substitute folder with pre-planned lessons and activities for those days when someone calls in sick at the last minute. Above all, remember that God works all things together for good to those who love Him (see Romans 8:28).

While you may not understand why plan A fell through, God can and will continue to work through your sincere efforts to continue to glorify Him and lead children closer to Him.

Day 31: Questions

1) How do you respond when you are faced with plan B?

2) What are three events or programs that you could prepare a plan B for in advance?

3) Prepare a plan B for each of those events.

Colección Filosofía y Teoría Políticas

dirigida por Fabián Ludueña Romandini

*La pregunta por el sentido de la política,
su alcance, su tradición y sus posibilidades
ha sido fundamental en las más diversas culturas.
La presente colección busca interrogarse sobre
el fenómeno de lo político atendiendo a
la pluralidad de perspectivas históricas y escuelas
teóricas. En igual medida, la política se encuentra
en asiduo contacto con otros saberes y prácticas
de cuya variedad también se querrá dar cuenta.
En la línea del legado de Hannah Arendt,
se trata de que los libros vayan tejiendo la trama
de investigaciones que, al mismo tiempo,
permita pensar en un nuevo mundo público común
frente a los desafíos crecientes de la política global
en el presente siglo.*

Cecilia Abdo Ferez

Libertad y cuerpo : Escapes de la libertad autoritaria presente

1ª ed. - Barcelona / Buenos Aires: Miño y Dávila editores - Junio 2025.

172 p.; 23x15 cm.

ISBN: 979-13-87546-11-3
E-ISBN: 979-13-87546-12-0
Depósito legal: M-10327-2025

Edición: Primera. Junio 2025
Lugar de edición: Barcelona, España / Buenos Aires, Argentina

Ilustración de portada: Benjamín Aitala, *S/T* [3671], Acrílico sobre tela, 100 x 70 cm. (2022).

ISBN: 979-13-87546-11-3
e-ISBN: 979-13-87546-12-0
Depósito legal: M-10327-2025

THEMA: QDTS [Social & political philosophy]
QÐT [Topics in philosophy]
BISAC: PHI019000 [Political]
IBIC: HPS [Filosofía social y política]
WGS: 710 [Social sciences, law, economy / Social sciences general]
6730 [Social sciences, law, economy / Political science]

Diseño: Gerardo Miño

Página web: www.minoydavila.com.ar

Mail: minoydavila@gmail.com

Dirección: Miño y Dávila s.r.l.
Tacuarí 540.
(C1071AAL), Buenos Aires
Whatsapp (+54 9 11) 6226-7681